Contents

INTRODUCTION 4
World water facts 6

COLLECTING AND STORING WATER 8
Containers 8
Other options 13

RETAINING WATER 16
Healthy soil 16
Mulches 17
Protecting plants 22

ECONOMIC WATERING 24
When to water 25
Utilising greywater 26
Watering by hand 27
Pitcher irrigation 28
Seep or soaker hoses 29
Drip irrigation 30
Pumps 31

JUDICIOUS PLANTING 32
Sowing seeds 32
Planting vegetables 33
Planting under plastic 36
Planting trees and shrubs 37
Planting annuals and perennials 38
Planting meadows 39

DROUGHT-RESISTANT PLANTS 40
Trees 42
Shrubs 46
Perennials 50
Annuals 54
Climbers and ground covers 56
Grasses 59
Herbs 60
List of drought-resistant plants 62

INDEX 64

INTRODUCTION

'Gardening without water' is in fact not possible. But gardening without expensive tap water is. In many parts of the world, water is already scarce and at a premium, and many western countries are now on metered water, the cost of which is rising. In the UK, most homes are still not metered, but this will surely change in the near future.

The gloomy fact is that the world *could* slowly but surely run out of water. In recent years, the demand for water has far outstripped the rate at which it can be replenished. World population is still rising, homes are acquiring more labour-saving machines, intensive farming is on the increase, and gardening is now one of the biggest growing leisure activities – all these facts contribute to the potential for an increasing water shortage almost everywhere.

We hear and read a great deal about global warming and energy saving but water shortage could actually become an even more pressing problem, with the result that water itself may soon be considered more precious than oil.

Mark Twain wrote, 'whiskey is for drinking, but water is worth fighting over'. He could hardly have known how true that might become one day. In the past, farmers and ranchers wrangled over water, but today water is already the source of many conflicts and legal actions.

At present, global warming is not actually reducing rainfall, but it is making weather patterns far more erratic. An area can go for many years with little rain and then have it all in one fell swoop. Recently, the south of England experienced several years of summer drought, followed by a summer of deluges. In the United States of America, California experienced a similar phenomenon – and the rain that followed the drought caused crops and houses to be swept away in a sea of mud. Not exactly the ideal gardening conditions!

Gardeners are at the worst end of this gloomy picture. Not only do they have to contend with erratic weather, but in times of drought they are the first to be hit – with hose pipe bans and even total bans on watering the garden from tap water

Gardening without
WATER

Creating beautiful gardens using only rainwater

CHARLOTTE GREEN

Henry Doubleday Research Association
SEARCH PRESS

First published in Great Britain 1999

Search Press Limited
Wellwood, North Farm Road,
Tunbridge Wells, Kent TN2 3DR

in association with

The Henry Doubleday Research Association
National Centre for Organic Gardening
Ryton-on-Dunsmore
Coventry CV8 3LG

ISBN 0 85532 855 1

Colour separation by P&W Graphics, Singapore
Printed in Spain by Elkar S. Coop. Bilbao 48012

The Author would like to thank the following:

Peter Beck for the use of the picture of *cercis siliquastrum* on page 43.

Martin Crawford of Agroforestry Research Trust of Totnes, Devonshire, England, for permission to use his database of drought-resistant plants.

Pat and Peter Donovan for supplying the plan of the Victorian storage tank on page 14.

Glen Haughton for demonstrating the planting pictures on pages 33 and 37.

Joyce, Ted and Philip Law for assisting in garden experiments.

Mary Ann Kunkel for supplying the picture of Clary sage on page 41.

Royal Botanical Gardens, Wakehurst Place, Sussex, England, for permission to photograph many of their beautiful plants.

Sue Turner, Head Gardener of HDRA Yalding, for information on plants grown at Yalding.

Cleve West and Johnny Woodford, Garden Designers of Teddington, Middlesex, England, who designed the Waterwise garden for Thames Water at the Hampton Court Flower Show 1998. Pictures of the garden appear on the front cover and on pages 4–5, page 20 (bottom left) and page 41 (bottom).

Very special thanks to:

Dr. Brian Arkell of the Environment Agency for reading and commenting on this book.

Peter Parker of the Centre of Alternative Technology, Wales, for much helpful advice on this book and for the use of the picture (bottom centre) on page 8 © Peter Parker 1999.

The Hon. Terry L. Underhill, horticu;turist, of Rattery, Devon, England, for invaluable help, especially with the drought-resistant plant lists.

Finally:

To Bill Loney who not only allowed me the freedom of his beautiful garden, 'Keppelcroft', in the Bruce Peninsula, Canada, but who might have written this book since he had already put into practice much of what is suggested here and who patiently answered endless questions.

Grateful thanks to many others who freely gave much help and advice.

The Publisher would like to thank the following:

Nigel Bateson for the iceberg photograph on pages 6–7, © 1999 Nigel Bateson.

Border Stone of Welshpool, Powys, Wales, for supplying the inert stone mulches on page 19.

Claymore Grass Machinery of Bidford-on-Avon, Warwickshire, England for the loan of the chipper/shredder on page 16.

Tony Hayes of Water Diverter of Croydon, Surrey, England, for providing the water diverter on page 11.

Hozelock Ltd of Aylesbury, Buckinghamshire, England, for supplying the soaker hose, timers and four-gang connectors on page 29.

Lizant Innovations of Newport, Isle of Wight, England, for the precision watering can on page 19.

Donald McIntyre, Countryside Advisor, Batheaston, Bath, England, for use of the wild meadow pictures on page 39, © Donald McIntyre 1999.

Melcourt Industries Ltd of Tetbury, Gloucestershire, England, for supplying the ornamental bark mulch on page 17 and subsequent pages.

Organic Gardening magazine for the idea of creating the water container from old car tyres, shown on page 10.

Prima Pots of Flimwell, Kent, England, for the unglazed pots on page 28.

Stuart Turner Ltd of Henley-on-Thames, Oxfordshire, England for supplying the pumps on page 31.

The United Nations Environment Programme for permission to quote the Chungungo story from *Taking Action – An Environmental Guide for You and Your Community* on page 7.

The University of Arizona Water Resources Research Center, USA and Purdue University Environmental Protection Agency, Indiana, for use of their cd's and discs.

supplies. This can be a nightmare for those who have striven to make a beautiful, peaceful haven round their house, or those who grow luscious fruit and vegetables. But – and here is the good news – you *can* beat the erratic weather and those droughts *and* any restrictions that may be imposed.

This is not a technical gardening book on how to grow, maintain and design gardens. It is a book that tells you not only how you can collect and store water, but how it can be used sparingly and with great effect. Even in deserts it rains, so no matter where you live it is possible to collect and store rainwater for use when it is most needed.

There is a chapter on how to best use your stored water with the help of many modern irrigation systems. Mulching, both with organic and inert materials is the basis of a plant's survival in dry conditions and this is covered extensively. Judicious planting is also extremely important. If planted in the right way, both fruit and vegetables will mature with little or no water.

An increasing number of articles and books are being published about water-wise gardens, rainwater gardens, low water gardens and xeriscape gardens (xeriscape was coined in the US from the Greek *xeros* meaning 'dry'). These largely deal with redesigning your garden and completely replanting it with drought-resistant plants. Most people will not want to uproot all their existing trees, shrubs and perennials, so I have tried to tell you how existing plants can survive.

As you slowly introduce new plants, you can refer to the lists and illustrations provided of trees, shrubs, flowers, climbers and herbs to see which will best survive in rainless conditions.

It does not matter where you live, you can always create and maintain a garden with beautiful plants and flowers.

World water facts

- Water is a precious *finite* resource, not infinite as many people suppose.

- The planet Earth abounds in water, yet only one per cent of it is 'sweet' (non-saline) and available for human, animal and plant consumption. The rest is locked up in salty oceans or in ice caps at the North and South poles.

- Remarkably, only about one per cent of the available sweet water (0.001% of total water) is actually used by humans for sustaining life. The average person drinks approximately 1–1.5 litres (2–3 US pints) per day.

- Average rainfall over the last ten to twenty years has neither increased nor decreased, despite the fact that weather patterns are becoming more erratic. However, in the same period, the demand for water has increased by approximately thirty per cent.

- Many areas in America already have a dire water shortage and experts are predicting that some states could run out of water by 2020.

- Many of the world's great rivers have been depleted out of all recognition. This has had drastic effects on the environment and the ecology of water systems.

- Approximately forty per cent of the world's population depends on water flowing from another country. The once mighty Colorado River supplies seven states in the USA and northern Mexico, and is now sometimes called a 'river of controversy'.

- Many communities use underground water supplies for drinkable water. This source was considered inexhaustible, but it is now threatened with depletion and contamination.

- The High Plains aquifer in the United States, known as the Ogallala, supplies water for irrigation from Minnesota to Texas. Extraction is vastly exceeding the rate at which it recharges, with the result that some land is no longer irrigated and, therefore, produces no more crops.

- The UK, generally considered a water-abundant country, only ranks thirty-seventh (out of one hundred and forty-nine countries) for the amount of annual renewable fresh water available per person. Ethiopia is next in the table with slightly more water per capita.

- Iceland has the greatest amount of annual renewable fresh water available per capita per year in the world.

- All the water that comes out of our taps (at least in the Western world) is treated, at great expense, to bring it up to drinking water standards. Nearly half of this water literally 'goes down the drain' by flushing toilets, and the other half by emptying baths, basins and sinks.

- Although statistics vary greatly, the average current use of water in European households is approximately 150 litres per person per day. In the USA it is three times as much (120 US gallons).

- Even if *all* leaks in water pipes were repaired, we would still need to conserve water and reduce the present rate of consumption.

- A leaking tap producing one drop per second, wastes 9000 litres (2400 US gallons) per year.

- Experts are predicting that in Great Britain, garden water consumption could double between 1990 and 2020. If the temperature rises by just 1°C (2°F), consumption could rise even more.

- Not all water facts are gloomy. New ideas for creating water supplies are being tried out in various parts of the world. Here is just one example that has proved very efective.

The village of Chungungo, in an arid region in Chile with no regular rainfall or rivers, had to obtain its water by road at great cost – US $8 per person per day. In 1987, Chilean Universities and the National Forestry Corporation, jointly initiated a 'fog trap' project to collect water:

'Fifty collectors, each measuring 48m² (520ft²), were erected above the town. The material used was a double-layer polypropylene mesh net, which costs little and is produced in Chile. The mesh collectors are entirely passive devices, requiring no energy. In addition, since collectors are normally situated on terrain higher than surrounding settlements, water can be delivered by gravity flow. The system gathers an average of 7200 litres (2000 US gallons) of water a day, a yield that was obtained even during three consecutive years of drought.'

The system still works today. The cost of water has been cut by seventy-five per cent, and for the first time in their history, villagers are cultivating family vegetable plots. This alternative water supply system is now widely used in other parts of Chile, in Peru and even in the Sultanate of Oman.

COLLECTING AND STORING WATER

There is only a handful of places in the world where it *never* rains. When it does rain, you should collect and save as much water as possible for, dare I say it, that 'rainy day'. It is surprising how much a relatively small roof area can collect over a year (see opposite).

(see opposite)

Warning
If small children have access to any stored water, make sure the lids or closures are child-proof.

Containers

Containers are excellent for collecting and storing water. There are many different types of proprietary water butts available, sized between 100–500 litres (25–125 US gallons).

The greenhouse pictured is fitted with a single plastic butt, but, if there is sufficient rainfall, several butts could be linked together on each side.

Wooden water butts, fitted with hand- or electrically-operated pumps, can be used as attractive garden features, but these can be rather expensive.

Plastic butt – capacity: 210 litres (55 US gallons)

Small plastic drum – capacity: 150 litres (40 US gallons)

Bulk orange juice container – capacity: 1500 litres (400 US gallons)

Oil tank – capacity: up to 10000 litres (2500 US gallons)

However, you can also use any number of other containers, some of which you can obtain at little or no cost.

Small plastic drums, used originally to contain food or chemicals, can often be obtained free of charge from manufacturers or wholesalers.

Larger containers, used to transport fruit pulp, for example, and capable of holding up to 1500 litres (400 US gallons), can also be obtained.

Old or new oil tanks, or similar containers, will also hold considerably more than an ordinary water butt – up to 10000 litres (2500 US gallons).

The number of containers or water butts required will be determined by the size of your garden and the weather conditions in your area. If you intend growing many vegetables, even in a small area, you will require considerably more water than the same area planted with only drought-resistant trees, shrubs and perennials. At the same time, no one can predict the exact rainfall or temperatures in any one year, so what might be sufficient one year may prove to be totally inadequate the next.

Relatively inexpensive kits are available for the collection and distribution of rainwater.

Reduce your water usage
You can save lots of household water by using the shower instead of taking baths.

Collecting roof water
The total amount of water you can collect from a roof in one year =

roof width x roof length x amount of annual rainfall

If you want to allow for evaporation, reduce this volume to 70%.

Cleaning containers
All old containers should be thoroughly cleaned and rinsed out to eliminate all residues, before filling with rainwater

Storing water You can use almost any container to store water, from an old bath or sink to a galvanised iron or plastic tank. If you think your containers look unsightly, why not decorate them with a coat or two of paint, or clothe them with attractive climbing plants.

Making a container

Old discarded car tyres can be used to make water storage containers. All you need are four to six ordinary car tyres and a large thick plastic sack or plastic liner. Use your ingenuity to make a lid.

Recycled containers
If buying commercial containers, try to obtain those made from recycled materials.

1. Use a sharp craft knife to cut round one tyre wall, halfway between the tread and the wire rim. Wetting the rubber with water will make this easier.

2. On the other side of the tyre, cut round the wall close to the tread. Turn the tyre inside out.

3. Repeat this sequence with several tyres, stack them and then line the inside with plastic.

Installing rainwater pipes

It is relatively simple to install a rainwater collection system to greenhouses, sheds and out-buildings which are not already fitted with guttering. All you need is a selection of the fittings shown here. These are available in various shapes, sizes and colours, and they normally snap together easily.

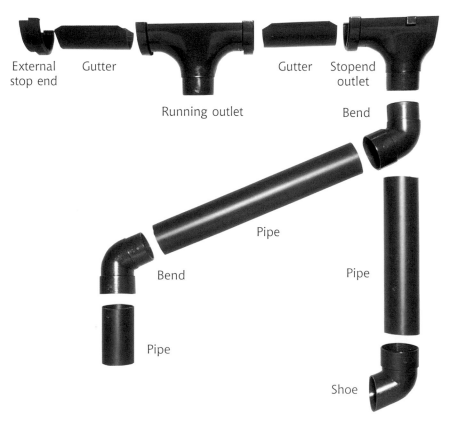

External stop end   Gutter

Running outlet

Gutter   Stopend outlet

Bend

Pipe

Bend   Pipe

Pipe

Shoe

Connecting fittings
If you have difficulty in connecting the fittings together, ease the corners on each end of gutters with a hacksaw.

Inserting a water-diverter

Most modern houses and garages have plastic rainwater gutters and downpipes. One of the best ways to collect rainwater is to install a diverter into a downpipe. There are many different types available – just make sure you get one the right size. Older houses may have cast iron guttering and downpipes, and you may need professional help to install diverters

1. Mark off the size of the diverter and remove a section of the downpipe with a hacksaw.

2. De-burr the edges to ensure a good, smooth fit.

3. Insert the diverter.

4. Connect the diverter to the container with a flexible hose.

5. Open the valve (if one is fitted).

Types of diverter
Some diverters work on a weir system, only diverting water until the butt is full. Excess water then runs back down the drain. Others, such as this example, have a valve system. When the valve is closed, all water is diverted to the butt. When the butt is full it will overflow, but it is better to use an overflow hose and direct the water on to plants rather than just let it disappear down the drain.

Warning
Do not cut into asbestos pipes, as this is a health hazard. Arrange to have them replaced professionally.

Leaks
Regularly check your plumbing system for leaks. Even a tiny leak can waste thousands of litres of water.

Linking water butts

You can attach a water butt to each downpipe on your rainwater guttering system. Alternatively, you could link several butts together, using as many as can be filled by your local rainfall. This is practical, but maybe not particularly aesthetic.

Most commercial water butts are supplied with taps, and some have fittings that enable you to join butts together. However, where such fittings are not supplied, separate kits are available and installation is quite easy. All you need is a drill and a drillbit of the correct size.

1. Drill an appropriate sized hole in your butt. Position the hole just below the top of the container for an overflow pipe. Position it near the bottom for a tap or linking connection.

2. Fit a hose/tank connector to the butt, sealing it with a washer and backnut. Then, fit the hose to the connector – softening the end of the hose in hot water will help get a good fit.

Linking butts The picture shows two butts linked together at the bottom. Note the overflow connections at the top of each butt. In this system the water level is the same in each tank, and one overflow hose need be connected. Overflow hoses should be directed straight on to the garden. Note also that the butts are mounted on a stout plinth above ground level, to allow waterering cans to be placed under the tap (shown at the extreme left).

Concrete tank This concrete underground storage tank holds 10000 litres (2500 US gallons) of water.

Well This is an old well still in use. New polythene pipes have been fitted that run underground to a pump in the basement of the house.

Restored well This well has had a new top built. It now needs a pump to extract the water (see page 31), and a lid to keep the water sweet and keep children out!

Other options

Cess pits and septic tanks

A number of houses now on mains drainage, have old disused cess pits or septic tanks. These could well be adapted to take any overflow from above-ground butts or containers. A simple overflow connection and a hose are quite adequate. Alternatively, plumb rainwater pipes into the original drainage system.

Arrange to have any old sludge pumped out professionally. Once the container is clean, fill it with water and use a good ecologically-sound cleaning agent to get rid of any remaining pathogens or bacteria.

Underground tanks and wells

Many Mediterranean countries, Australia and some states in America still have rainwater storage systems in use today. (I am told in Australia they use the tap water for irrigation and the rainwater for washing and drinking!) In more northerly countries, like the UK, many Victorian homes were built with underground rainwater storage tanks, or they had wells somewhere in the garden. It is amazing how many such wells and tanks I have found in my neighbourhood! These can easily be restored and resurrected, provided you fit an adequate pump (see page 31). My own home has no mains water but is supplied by a natural spring. A previous owner had thousands of intensively farmed chickens who apparently drank the spring dry during rainless summer months. I unearthed no less than three holding tanks, all of which were totally overgrown.

Building an underground tank

If your search for a well or disused underground system is unsuccessful and you find endless butts a bit unsightly, consider building an underground tank of your own. (Check with your local Council whether you will need planning permission.)

Nowadays, with plenty of labour-saving machinery for hire, it need not be horrendously time-consuming or expensive. However, *unless you know exactly what you are doing*, consult a builder or expert. The materials and thickness of walls must be sufficiently strong to withstand all kinds of pressure, especially on clay soils.

Victorian storage tank

This diagram shows an existing Victorian storage tank. You could adapt the design, but again, *be careful*, and consult an expert: you do not want to undermine your home's foundations! If you keep an eye on the tank, you can cut off the overflow: disconnect the hose, or make sure that you shut off the valve if you have cut into a downwater pipe. Better still, direct the overflow straight on to the garden. This, and indeed any other underground storage tank or pond, will require a pump (see page 31).

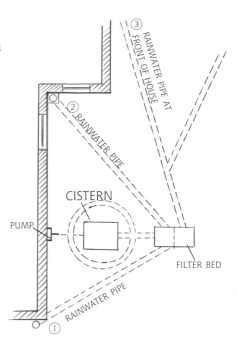

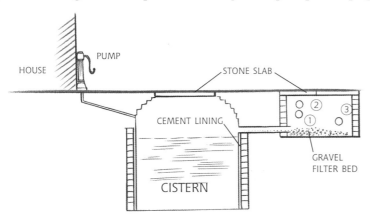

Ponds

If you are lucky enough to have a large natural pond, you can pump out some of the water when conditions get really dry (see page 31).

Garden pond You can extract water from a pond, but you should always make sure you leave enough to sustain any wildlife.

Linking ponds These rocks form the link between the three ponds featured in the photograph on the right.

If you do not have a pond, it is quite possible to build one, or even a series of ponds. The pond should be supplied directly from a convenient rainwater source, or from the overflow of water butts. Whilst it is beyond the scope of this small book to tell you how to construct a pond, there are plenty of books and water garden centres where you can find help and advice.

The problem with ponds is that in absolutely no time you will probably find them teeming with all kinds of wildlife, which can present you with a difficult decision if you want to extract water. By some kind of miracle, wild water plants appear, and with them frogs, toads, dragon flies, damsel flies and a host of other animals and insects. Even fish have been known to appear apparently out of nowhere. Think carefully before pumping out the water from such a pond. Make sure you leave sufficient water for all these creatures and plants to survive.

Vegetation These three small ponds are entirely supplied with water from a garage roof. The impressive vegetation – much of which arrived uninvited – has almost completely covered one of the ponds.

Purpose-built pond This large purpose-built water storage pond has a storm drain at the far end.

15

RETAINING WATER

There are many ways of protecting plants and retaining moisture. The most important are creating and maintaining a humus-rich soil, and practising constant mulching.

Healthy soil

A good living soil, rampant with earthworms and micro-organisms, is all-important if you want plants to succeed with little or no water. Humus, leaf mould and/or compost should be forked in regularly. This will increase the soil's water-retention capabilities enormously, improve its structure and drainage and ensure strong, healthy plants. Humus and compost can retain up to eighty or ninety per cent water. A clay soil, said to be the most water retentive, only holds fifteen to twenty per cent.

There will be far less chance of success if the soil has only had chemical fertilisers, herbicides and pesticides (which inhibit the natural beneficial organisms) poured into it rather than humus. At worst the soil will go as hard as rock, or turn into dust and erode. This is true for whatev type of soil you have.

There are many ways to make compost and humus. Details can be found in many books, including one in this series entitled *All about Compost*. If you cannot make sufficient compost or leaf mould from your garden, buy manure from farms and stables. You should also contact local council recycling centres; they often give away leaf mould or compost.

Composting All organic waste and animal manure can be composted fairly quickly in a home-made container, bin, or just a heap. Make sure everything is mixed up well and turned as often as possible.

Leaf mould Leaves can be collected and put in a wire container or plastic sack. When rotted down, they can be dug in or used as a surface mulch. Leaf mould is not as rich as compost.

Hedge clippings and prunings If you have a fair-sized garden, you will probably have a lot of clippings and prunings, especially in autumn. These can be chopped and put on the compost heap, where, unfortunately they may take several years to rot. If possible, buy a decent-sized chipper/shredder – you will find it invaluable. The resultant shreddings can be composted more quickly, or used as a mulch round shrubs and trees. Do not shred green laurel leaves as they give off a poisonous vapour; wait until they turn brown.

Compost and/or animal manure

Grass mowings

Cocoa shell

Coarse bark

Straw

Leaf mould

Woodchips

Hay

Shredded clippings

Mulches

Good mulching over wet soil is the secret of maintaining a garden with little or no water. You can use both organic and inorganic mulches. You will be amazed at how long a 10–12cm (4–5in) deep mulch (be it compost, leaf mould, mowings, pebbles or stones) can keep the soil moist, even in very hot, dry conditions.

Organic mulches

Compost, leaf mould and composted shreddings can all be used as surface mulches, as well as to enrich the soil. You can also use other organic materials. Excess mowings make a wonderful moisture-retaining mulch for both fruit, vegetables and other plants. Mowings can also be mixed into your compost heap or they can be left on the lawn itself as a mulch.

Bark, wood chips and cocoa shell are more permanent organic mulches and are therefore good for perennials, trees and shrubs.

Deep grass mulch All vegetables benefit from deep grass mulches. In fact, some people living in dry areas believe it is the best way to grow all vegetables. Here, runner beans and Swiss chard are mulched with grass mowings.

Working worms
Worms work hard to transport organic mulches into the soil. So, no matter how you use them, over time, organic mulches will end up looking much the same as the soil.

Grass mulch Fennel will thrive if planted in a mulch of grass mowings.

Grass mulch Peas like the moisture of a grass mulch.

Compost and hay mulch These raspberry canes are in a good mulch of compost and hay.

Bark Mulch *Phormium tenax* with a heavy bark mulch.

Grass mulch These young cucumbers are great guzzlers of both water and food, so a good mulch and plenty of compost will help.

Leaf mould mulch This young *Choisya ternata* 'Sundance' is mulched with leaf mould. This variety is not only a wonderful golden colour but is also scented.

Suppressing weeds

You can put newspaper, cardboard, permeable plastic or old carpet underneath any surface mulch – this will not only suppress weeds, but will also help keep in extra moisture. This technique is best used for trees, shrubs and perennials.

Inert mulches

A salient feature of all low-water gardens is inert mulches, i.e. stones, gravel, rocks and pebbles. Unlike organic mulches, these are more or less permanent and therefore careful thought must be given before using them. A combination of inert mulches can be used to create many designs in your garden, so do not rush out to buy anything before deciding exactly what effect you want to achieve.

Limestone chipping — Golden flint — Pearl spar — Grey granite grit — Gravel mix (small) — Red granite chipping — Gravel mix (medium) — Limestone chipping — Gravel mix (large) — Marble/limestone chipping

Background: Black and white spar

Multi-coloured inert mulches This medieval-type garden has been created with multi-coloured inert mulches where once there was a lawn. The planting is not yet complete but it will eventually consist of *Artemisias, Sempervivums, Sedums* and an *Agave* in the centre.

Gravel mulch These yuccas are planted in a thick gravel mulch.

Local stones *Abies concolor* and other trees are here planted among local stones.

Collecting your own inert mulches

Before going out to purchase inert mulches from garden centres, try digging in your own garden – some grounds are naturally stoney, whereas others may have sandstone or limestone some way below the surface. Stunning effects can be achieved with pebbles, stones, rocks and gravel, whether dug up from your garden or purchased, so let your imagination run wild.

Rock feature The tightly-packed rosettes of this *Sempervivum* are surviving in a mere indent in a large rock.

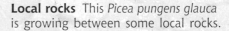

Local rocks This *Picea pungens glauca* is growing between some local rocks.

Knot gardens The D's in the above design are from Henry **D**ouble**D**ay and are *Buxus sempervirens suffriticosa*. The garden to the right is a seventeenth-century Knot garden with *Santolina viridis* and *S. chamaecyparissus* planted in pea gravel mulch.

Protecting plants

Whether introducing new plants or maintaining old ones, think about protecting them. Direct hot sun all day will soon dry out soil, and any kind of wind can also devastate. Walls, fences or hedges will provide both a windbreak and shade for some of the day.

Fences and walls

Sue Stickland, in her book *The Small Ecological Garden* (HDRA and Search Press, 1996), gives the following advice:

'The best windbreak effect is provided by those barriers that filter rather than block the wind: ideally they should be about fifty per cent holes. Solid walls and fences and very dense hedges can cause damaging eddies on the leeward side. On a sloping site they can also trap cold air and create frost pockets. Hedges, walls and fences will give shelter over a distance of about six to eight times their height, so one that is 1.5–1.8m (5–6ft) tall round the boundary of a small garden gives good protection.'

The position of your house and the direction of prevailing winds will largely determine where you build any wall or fence, or plant hedges. Also consider what you want to grow. For instance, fruits such as loganberries, tayberries, blackberries and espalier fruits, will appreciate a wall or fence. Many vegetables, such as brassicas, will welcome shade from the hottest sun, whilst many flowers will love to be in full sun.

Drought-resistant hedges

Hedges not only provide a haven for birds and wildlife, and shade and protection for many plants, but there are a number of hedging plants that are attractive in themselves. Many varieties are drought-resistant and some of these are shown on the page opposite.

An effective windbreak A fence woven from natural hazel or willow stems makes a good windbreak.

Disguising walls Walls can be clothed with living colour, as this purple ivy shows.

Filtering wind These two fences, above and below, have gaps to filter the wind and so avoid turbulence. This set-up works well for all kinds of fruit.

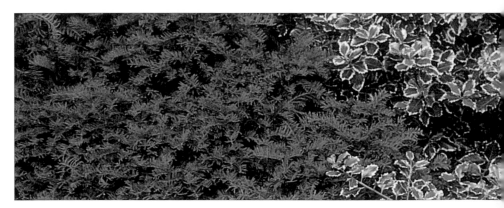

Yews, junipers and hollies These can make good, plain classic-looking hedges. The photograph below shows an unusual combination of *Taxus baccata, Ilex aquifolium variegata* and *Juniperus spp.*

Viburnum opulus This flowers in spring, with vibrantly coloured berries and foliage in autumn.

Ligustrum vulgare This can provide a home and food for the spectacular Privet moth lavae.

Euonymus europaeus Spindle trees are good for alkaline soils, and birds love the red seed berries.

Taxus baccata Yew is slow growing but gives good protection. Many golden varieties are available. The berries are poisonous.

Ilex aquifolium Holly has insignificant flowers, but attractive berries in the autumn and winter for birds and Christmas decorations.

Crataegus monogyna This has spring and autumn interest. It flowers in spring and has berries in autumn that birds love.

ECONOMIC WATERING

It is summer and there is no rain, only hot sun. If you have planted everything correctly (see page 32–39), only minimal watering should be necessary.

Before doing so, think about how plants behave and why they need water. Light and water are two essentials for the well-being of all plants. They use both to perform that wonderful process called photosynthesis – that is, they take in carbon dioxide and give out pure oxygen. Plants also take in water through their roots, but then give it off in vapour form through their leaves – this is called transpiration. The higher the temperature, the more water transpires. To make matters worse, water also evaporates from the soil, especially in hot and windy conditions.

Given half the chance, plants, like most humans, will take the easy short-term option. Watering dry soil with a sprinkler or hose will make plants spread their roots near the surface where they will only find temporary relief. It is better if they are forced to search for moisture further down. So, educate your plants and help them develop long, deep roots (some, like poppies, develop long tap roots naturally) by watering correctly – that is, with a can directly down to the roots. Once well established, many plants, even water-loving ones, can resist drought if proper care and attention has been given to correct planting and watering.

If possible, water your plants before sunrise when the soil is cool!

- Never use sprinklers – too much water evaporates in the air and water does not get directly to roots.

- Overwatering plants can be as damaging as a complete lack of water.

- Make sure plants really need water. If uncertain, purchase a moisture meter and follow the manufacturer's instructions.

- Do not use a watering can with a rose (except for seeds).

- Do not overwater seedlings – it can cause 'damping off'.

- Simple clockwork timers enable you to water while you are asleep when the soil is at its coolest.

Transpiration

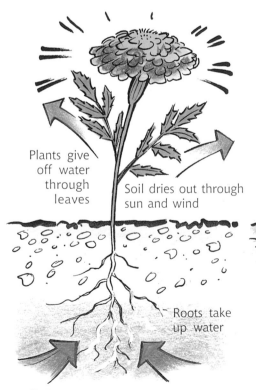

Plants give off water through leaves

Soil dries out through sun and wind

Roots take up water

The effect on the soil and plants if you use sprinklers and roses

Fine sprinkle

Wet soil

Dry soil

Wet soil

When to water

Autumn and winter

You should not have to water at all during autumn or winter. Many perennials die down completely, and trees and shrubs (even conifers and evergreens) take a rest. The sap no longer runs up their branches, and only minimal transpiration takes place.

Spring and summer

If spring is very dry, you may have to give some water to young plants, but if the soil has been properly prepared and young seedlings planted correctly (see pages 32-35), the ground should still have sufficient moisture to get them going. With any luck, spring bulbs, especially woodland ones, should have looked after themselves during the preceding months and they should burst into bloom with no further attention.

Bulbs
Naturalised daffodils and crocuses will automatically appear in spring, unless you live in a desert or arid region.

Weeds

Whatever the season, but especially when water is in short supply, weeds fight fiercely for survival and will quickly and voraciously seek out any available moisture, leaving your favourite specimens high and dry! Many have even devised special ways of growing in dry weather and they adapt far quicker to changing conditions than cultivated plants. These plants must be kept under control if water is to be retained in the soil for the plants you are trying to grow. Mulching with either organic or inert materials will keep most weeds under control. The addition of newspaper, cardboard or plastic under the mulch will make it even more effective.

Utilising greywater

Greywater (or gray water) is the term usually applied to water from baths, showers, sinks and washing machines. The terms reclaimed, silver- and greenwater have also crept into our vocabulary. Estimates vary, but of the total amount of water used, the average household produces approximately forty-five percent of greywater. The term blackwater is applied to water which comes from toilets (sewage) and this accounts for a minimum of thirty-five per cent of all water usage.

As so much greywater goes down the drain, it can and should be recycled and used together with rainwater to supply much of our garden needs. However, virtually no research has been done on the effects that chemicals and human pathogens present in greywater can have on the soil and plants. Legislation on greywater usage is 'murky' to say the least! In the US, many states still ban its use for irrigation unless treated, despite the acute shortage in some states. Britain currently has no regulations, and no two European countries seem to have identical policies.

In the absence of any information, I decided to try my own limited experiment to establish how plants and the soil react to the worst possible form of greywater. I chose my kitchen sink and dishwater full of grease and cleaning agents, and emptied it on to a northeast-facing triangular shrubbery/flower bed.

Fortunately the drain pipe was plastic, so cutting into it was easy. During that summer there was virtually no rain, so a hose was moved around the bed for nine months and the soil and plants had to absorb everything my drains threw at them. By the following spring I expected all sorts of trouble: distorted growths . . . no flowers . . . On the contrary, everything thrived and still is thriving. However, this was purely an experiment, and I would advise that you use the cleaner greywater from baths, showers and basins.

After setting up my own experiment, I discovered *Gray Water Use in the Landscape*. Its author, Robert Kourik, had been a lone voice and

Greywater can feed plants Many cleaning agents contain phosphates, potassium and other minerals advantageous to plants.

Diverting water with a hose Bath or shower water can be diverted into a flexible hose.

Diverting water with a plastic bottle Downpipes can be modified, and with a simple plastic water bottle, greywater can be diverted directly on to the garden.

Greywater bed After nine months of constant greasy greywater, this bed of camellias, an azalea, cotoneaster, berberis, fuchsia, bergenia, ferns and even wild cyclamens still thrives two and three years later.

experimenter for many years. He clearly shows how plants cope with and even thrive on greywater. I had used only ecologically friendly powders, and if you intend using greywater you should try to do so too. Soaps are usually fairly harmless, but it is best to buy natural ones. As Kourik says, 'You must get back to basics, and only use simple soaps, detergents and "elbow grease" . . . Avoid all modern detergents with claims of softening, whitening and "enzymatic" powers, as well as bleaches in all forms. Especially harmful are cleansers or detergents with boron, a substance which can quickly build up to toxic levels . . . The salts that might build up from water are, in my experience, seldom a problem and are leached away by each heavy rain.'*

Unfortunately, plumbing practices vary from country to country, so how you plumb into your greywater will also vary. Fortunately, in Britain most pipes are outside, so tapping into them is relatively easy and inexpensive (see also pages 10 and 11).

Many systems are coming on to the market which automatically treat and recycle greywater for use in the house or garden. They are still relatively expensive but prices will fall in time.

Important points
- Avoid storing untreated greywater – use it directly on the garden.
- Do not use greywater on vegetables or fruit.
- It is best to avoid greywater from greasy kitchen sinks, and water from the first cycle of washing or dishwashing machines.
- Avoid the possible build-up of chemicals by not continually using greywater on the same patch of ground.

* By kind permission from *Gray Water Use in the Landscape* by Robert Kourik (Metamorphic Press © 1988, PO Box 1841, Santa Rosa, Ca 95402, USA)

Watering by hand

There are umpteen methods and irrigation systems for watering the garden. Unless you have a very large garden, the simple methods like hand watering and pitcher irrigation are best.

Hand watering can be tedious but it is an easy trouble-free method. If possible, purchase a watering can with a control valve. Make sure plants do really need water: slight wilting under direct sun does not necessarily mean that they must have it.

Correct watering Water directly to the roots, preferably with a can that has a control valve.

Incorrect watering Improper watering can result in roots running along the surface and being exposed to sun and wind.

Watering with a hose An espalier fruit tree is watered here with a hose. You might need a pump to get this sort of pressure. Always use hoses with controls at hand level and not at source.

Pitcher irrigation

This is a cheap, almost foolproof irrigation system which has been developed for crops in India. I experimented with lettuces, but there is no reason why you cannot use it on any water-loving vegetables.

This method has the added advantage that you can go away for a week or more (depending on the size of the pots) without having to worry about your plants. You must use *unglazed* clay pots with no holes in the bottom, and a lid. Pots without holes are expensive to buy, so make some by using cheap unglazed flower pots and a good waterproof glue. Use your ingenuity to make some sort of lid. I made crude wooden ones from pallet off-cuts.

The temperature during the growing period was up to 30°C (86°F), and I found that I had to fill each pot approximately every ten days. Each one held 5 litres (1 gallon) when full and I used a total of 50 litres (10 gallons) – considerably less than if I had watered with a can. This method produces a quick crop, but remember, with no water they would still have matured, but over a much longer period.

1. Put plenty of waterproof glue on to a crock.

2. Press the crock firmly into the bottom of a pot and leave to dry/harden.

3. Plant young seedlings around each sunken pot. Fill the pots with water and cover.

Pitcher-irrigated lettuces These lettuces were watered, as described above. This photograph was taken after seven weeks.

Seep or soaker hoses

This is another simple watering method. There are many types of seep or soaker hose, but they all work on the principle of dribbling water out through a succession of tiny holes. Most of them will work off the taps on water butts or containers, providing the butt is above ground level. You can either lay them straight along rows or snake them in and out of plants. They should be run *under* a mulch – a light one such as hay or straw is best.

Alternatively you can dig hoses into the ground. Many manufacturers claim they are frost proof and can be left in permanently. I would advise against this, especially in the vegetable garden where you will find them a nuisance when weeding or digging up root vegetables.

Check periodically for blockages in the tiny holes. It is a good idea to filter the water before it goes into the hose. You can put a mesh filter on to the outlet of your container, or buy one that fits into the hose.

You can even fit a timer to a water butt or container. A simple battery-operated one is best. Set the timer, fit it to the tap and then leave the tap open for the timer to start the flow of water. All being well, you can water your plants in the middle of the night! Try to estimate how much water the plants need and how long you should leave it running.

Water pressure
When attaching any kind of hose to a container tap, you must ensure there is sufficient head or pressure to force the water through the hose. The higher the container is above the ground, the greater the pressure. Alternatively, you can pump out the water (see page 31).

Soaker hose This soaker hose has been run under a mulch of straw.

Four-gang connector
Connectors enable you to water more than one row or bed at a time using seep or soaker hoses.

Timers A water butt can be fitted with a battery timer, a length of ordinary hose, then a soaker hose.

Drip irrigation

A drip irrigation system, either laid on the surface of the soil, or actually dug in, is one of the best water-conserving methods available. However, it is also a minefield: there are a plethora of products available, from simple do-it-yourself kits to sophisticated computer-operated systems. It is far beyond the scope of this book to adequately cover drip irrigation – there are whole tomes written on the subject.

I do not use any form of drip irrigation, despite having a large garden, and rely solely on mulching, watering cans and soaker hoses. I do, however, have a pump to bring up water from a pond and underground storage when necessary.

Most drip irrigation consists of a hose or pipe, on to which is attached a dripper which can be used singly or via a manifold with several drippers, enabling many pots or plants to be watered from one outlet.

When deciding upon a drip irrigation system, bear in mind the following points:

- Be absolutely sure what you want out of the system before purchasing anything.

- Make sure a good filter is installed. The filter on the pump prevents debris going down the line, but not tiny particles or algae which come from ponds or containers and are apt to clog the drippers.

- If you are installing anything but a tiny system, buy hoses that are pressure-compensated, that is, hoses with individual valves to ensure the same amount of water will go through each dripper.

- Buying an inexpensive system does not necessarily save money in the long run.

- Regularly inspect the 'line', clean it out and flush it if necessary.

Manifolds You can water several plants or pots from one dripper outlet via a manifold.

Single drippers   Manifold

Single dripper A single dripper can easily be attached to a hose.

A sump for that special tree or shrub

You can make a simple sump for any favourite trees, shrubs or perennials, especially those under a thick mulch and still getting themselves established (where possible, install a sump when planting). Take a length of piping or plastic tubing approximately 30–45cm (12–18in) long and make a few holes in the bottom. Insert it through the mulch, into the soil and near to the roots – this will be to a depth of 15cm–30cm (6–12in) depending on the size of the plant. Water through the top of the tube to ensure constant moisture round the roots. You can also fill the pipe with gravel so water does not 'rush' down. A steady hand and/or a can with a control valve is essential if watering through a sump.

Pumps

Once you get into pumps and irrigation systems, you could be digging deep into your pocket, as well as getting 'knee deep in hot water'! Pumps are necessary if you use water stored underground or from ponds and wells, or if you intend installing any type of sophisticated irrigation system. You can either buy a normal or submersible pump. The operation of both is similar, but a submersible has the advantage that it can be left *in situ*. The other type must be housed inside and plumbed accordingly. Both require a power point nearby.

Pumps can be expensive, so determine exactly what you want to achieve before you go and buy one. There are many considerations, including:

- How far is the water source from the plants?

- Is it up or downhill?

- How large is the area you want to water?

- Do you just want to replenish your water butts, or do you want to run an irrigation system?

- What pressure is ideal for your irrigation system?

- Make sure your water is filtered.

When you are sure what type will suit you, consult an expert and then follow the manufacturers' instructions. Alternatively, you can employ an irrigation specialist who will, at a price, install the pumps and irrigation systems.

Ordinary pump Water is pumped out of a large plastic storage tank by an ordinary pump. The electrics have to be housed in a waterproof place. The pump should be stored away when not in use.

Submersible pump This submersible pump is in a concrete underground storage tank. The pump can be kept in the water but the electrical control units must be housed somewhere waterproof.

Keeping the filter clean Always make sure the filter is kept free from debris and leaves.

Disguising hoses Pipes and hoses running above ground from storage tanks to various parts of the garden, can be unsightly and a nuisance. You can dig them in and fit couplings at different locations. Make sure they have a lid.

Timers
All pumps can be fitted with simple or sophisticated timers which will water at a certain time every night for a fixed period.

Pumping by hand If your pumps are clogged, your fuses are blown, your pipes and hoses are leaking and you are about to have a nervous breakdown, you can always pump by hand!

JUDICIOUS PLANTING

In the second chapter I stressed how important it was to have not only a good humus-rich soil, but also plenty of compost and mulches available to keep it moist. Now is the time to use them. You should use grass mowings, leaf mould, and hay or straw when planting out vegetables. Remember also, that it can take several years before soil reaches its peak water-retaining capabilities and that compost/humus/manure should be added annually. Always plant trees, shrubs and perennials in the autumn or rainy season to give them a good start in moist soil.

Sowing seeds

Germinating seeds do not need a rich compost, as they manufacture their own nutrients when forming. Moisture, however, is important but even here the amount of water given can be minimised.

Making plastic tunnels Some vegetables and annuals do not like being transplanted, so sow them under plastic tunnels. Moisture will form inside the tunnel – this is part condensation, part transpiration. The amount of moisture that forms in the tunnel and runs down the sides is usually sufficient to keep the seedlings at the sides moist. Do not sow down the centre of the tunnel unless you are able to water it. Most root vegetables like carrots, parsnips, turnips etc. and spinach do not like being transplanted.

Making a propagator This 'propagator' is a plastic drinks bottle cut in half. The upper half of the bottle generates moisture for the seeds.

Covering with plastic wrap If you sow seeds into pots, cover with plastic wrap. The moisture that this will generate is usually sufficient to germinate the seeds. If sowing seeds in conventional trays or wooden boxes, ensure they are covered with newspaper or plastic to retain moisture. If the soil dries out, you could damage tiny seedlings if you use a watering can – use a mist spray instead.

Potting on It is better to pot on seedlings into small containers, and only plant them out when they are a reasonable size. This will give them a better chance of surviving dry conditions. The photograph shows a selection of plants in recycled plastic pots, instead of conventional clay and plastic flower pots.

Planting vegetables

Most fruit and vegetables require moisture to mature and ripen, but much can be done to minimise watering if care is taken when planting. If possible, plant out strong, healthy, potted-on vegetables. These will have a good chance of surviving even without further watering. Certain families of vegetables require more water than others, but unfortunately there are no drought-resistant varieties available – so far.

1. Dig a small deep hole in prepared humus-rich soil.

2. Fill the hole with compost and mix well with the soil.

3. Saturate the hole with water.

4. Gently insert the plant, making sure the roots go to the bottom of the hole.

5. Cover with soil and press down.

6. Mulch the surface round the plant with any organic material – such as compost, grass mowings, hay or straw – to retain moisture.

Beds

I have no doubt that the best way to grow vegetables in dry conditions is on beds. This method has many advantages:

- It is not necessary to dig.

- Precious mulches are never wasted.

- You can always keep soil mulched tidily without it spreading on to paths.

- It is much easier to keep out weeds.

- Seedlings can be planted closer together in groups (rather than rows), which, once they are established will shade soil and keep in moisture.

- The growing area is much larger than in a plot planted in conventional rows.

- It is easy to plan a rotation system.

Self-sown vegetables

I often allow vegetables to seed themselves. This can only be done on beds. For some reason, the seedlings that spring up in their own time and place are far healthier and rarely get attacked by slugs. The varieties that have worked well for me include parsley, lettuces, asparagus, garlic and tomatoes in the greenhouse. It may not be as tidy, but it is more successful than sowing and planting out seedlings.

Plant close together These cos lettuces were closely planted in a well composted bed and never watered. They grew for approximately nine weeks, developed good hearts and then it rained. Sudden rain makes lettuces inclined to bolt, so these had to be eaten quickly!

Brassicas Most brassicas are greedy feeders. Here are some young ones growing in a well mulched and composted bed.

Heavy mulching Young runner beans (above) respond well to a heavy straw mulch.

Perfect potatoes The potatoes in these two photographs were planted in a bed of rich soil. They were covered with fairly clean, strawy animal bedding when about 20cm (8in) tall. They were never watered and it only rained a little in early spring. The harvest was excellent.

Planting under plastic

Personally, I do not like using plastics in or on the soil. In time it breaks down and leaves 'bits' floating around the garden. However, permeable plastic sheets are very useful in the vegetable garden – they control all weeds, let in rain and retain moisture well. You can purchase long rolls about the width of a bed. Protective, lightweight fleeces are good for spreading over plants. These will keep out some pests and retain moisture.

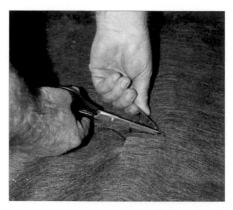

1. Spread permeable plastic over a moist, well-mulched bed, and cut small crosses where you want to plant.

2. Place the crown at soil level and then firm down the soil around the seedling.

Types of plastic There are several types of plastic suitable for planting under. This picture shows woven plastic, permeable sheet and ordinary plastic. The first two are preferable as they both let in water.

Row of shrubs This row of *Amelanchier canadensis* was planted under plastic several years ago and is well-established. The plastic should now be removed.

Permeable plastic mulch Strawberries are an exceptionally good crop to plant through plastic. The plastic will keep out weeds and keep the fruit clean. If you think the plastic looks unattractive, cover it with a fine bark mulch.

Protecting vegetables Young vegetables can be protected from slugs and kept moist with this mini greenhouse made from a plastic drinks bottle with the bottom cut out.

Planting trees and shrubs

The main thing to remember about trees and shrubs is that they are permanent – you can therefore use any of the organic or inert mulches. Wood chips are used in this demonstration, but gravel, crushed stones or pebbles may look even better.

1. Dig a big hole. If you have a clay soil, break up the sides and bottom to help drainage.

2. Add plenty of soil conditioners, such as leaf mould or compost.

3. Mix everything well and water thoroughly.

4. Plant the tree or shrub (this one is *Acer ginnala*) and press down the soil.

5. Stake and tie the tree (old tights are used here to secure the young trunk).

6. Cut a hole in some thoroughly wetted cardboard or make a ring of sheets of wet newspaper and place this round the plant.

7. Cover with at least 8–12cm (3–5in) of woodchip or bark. Alternatively, use an inert mulch such as gravel or stone.

Run-off planting

This method is used in many countries subject to prolonged periods of drought. It is useful for shrubs and trees, but can also help vegetables and other small plants.

Dig a 'bowl', plant a shrub and then add compost and/or mulch. This method ensures that when it does rain, all the water falling into the bowl will run down to the roots. It makes a wide catchment area for each plant.

Planting annuals and perennials

Annuals should be planted in the same way as vegetables. Try to choose drought-resistant varieties (see pages 40-61). Plant closer than normal so they give each other shade and reduce evaporation.

Perennials should be planted in a similar way to trees and shrubs (see previous page). However, initially, rather than using bark or an inert mulch, add a thick layer of compost, grass mowings or shreddings. This will rot and allow plants to spread in the following year when they will benefit from a further mulch round the shoots. Plant perennials in well-prepared beds.

Stone mulch These clumps of *Agapanthus* are planted in a mulch of local stone.

Stone mulches This path is mulched with stones and planted with a creeping juniper.

Leaf mould This mixed bed of drought-resistant plants has been heavily mulched with leaf mould.

Planting meadows

Lawns are wonderful in a garden. They are great to sit, lie and play on, and many people have them just because they think they are less work than flower beds or vegetables. It is amazing how many people, even those living in quite arid areas, insist on having them. This not only results in a vast array of chemical lawn products catering for every situation, but also a lot of water being wasted by sprinklers. *More water is expended on lawns than on any other part of the garden.*

So, why not plant a meadow instead, or at least make part of the lawn into one? You will be surprised at the number of pretty wild flowers that quickly establish themselves. Those that appear by themselves will be best suited to your soil and climate. There are numerous wild flower seeds available. Choose ones suitable for your soil and follow sowing instructions carefully. The plants may be wild, but they can often be more difficult to grow than cultivated plants. A wild meadow should be cut down to 5–8cm (2–3in) in late autumn once the seeds have set and dispersed.

If you must have a lawn

- Try to avoid having a manicured, bowling-green type lawn. Let it grow at least 5–10cm (2–4in) tall.

- The longer grass, the more shade is provided for the soil. Hence more moisture is retained in the soil.

- If grass turns brown, it does not mean it has died – it will spring into life when it rains.

- Mulch the lawn frequently with mowings or leaf mould.

- Try sowing a lawn with drought-resistant grasses such as fine fescues, rye grasses and Kentucky bluegrass.

Wild flower seeds

Make sure that any wild flower seeds you buy are just indigenous varieties and not mixed with imported ones.

Flower meadow This meadow is planted with flowers which are particularly suited to poor, chalky soils. It includes yarrow, vetches, oxeye daisies, birdsfoot trefoil, buttercups and many others.

DROUGHT-RESISTANT PLANTS

The fact that a plant is drought-resistant or completely frost-hardy does not necessarily mean it will survive in all conditions. Some which thrive in relatively dry but temperate climes may well not withstand the heat of desert conditions and vice versa. The plants listed on the following pages are only a fraction of the thousands that will survive in dry conditions. Before embarking on buying and planting expensive specimens, it is worth seeking the advice of your local garden centre, or a really good gardening encyclopaedia. Many will argue that the best and safest course is to grow only native plants. This is extremely good advice, but what if the climate in your area is changing?

You can often tell whether a plant will be drought-resistant by its appearance. Some have developed mechanisms in their leaves and roots to beat drought. Poppies, for example, have very long tap roots, whilst other plants turn their leaves away from the sun and even shed them and carry on the life-giving process of photosynthesis through their barks. The more easily recognisable drought-resistant plants are succulents, hairy plants and aromatic plants.

Plant names
The plants on the following pages in most cases only bear the botanical names. The common names vary greatly from area to area and country to country, and sometimes one plant can have eight to ten names. So, for the sake of space, we have only given the universally recognised botanical names.

Succulents These are easily recognised by their thick fleshy leaves which are used to store water. Apart from the obvious cacti, this group includes sempervivums, sedums, yuccas, aloes and many others. Cacti not only store water in their thick bodies and branches, but deflect the heat with their prickly spines.

Hairy plants Most plants whose leaves appear to be grey or white are drought-resistant. Many are not really grey, but are covered in a multitude of fine hairs which protect them from wind and sun and actually trap moisture. The middle leaf has been thoroughly soaked in water to illustrate it is really green. Other leaves, like those of poppies, appear green but are nevertheless covered in hairs.

Aromatic plants The volatile oil in aromatic leaves helps retain moisture by generating a protective haze around the plants. This makes trees (such as members of the enormous eucalyptus family) and most herbs drought-resistant.

Excessive rain If the structure and drainage of the soil is good, you should have no problems with drought-resistant plants, even if it rains excessively. Excessive rain can produce some strange results. Have you ever seen Clary sage *(Salvia sclarea)* compete with trees? This photograph shows Clary sage growing in a normally very arid area of Spain that was suddenly subjected to torrential rains and floods.

A drought-resistant border This border consists solely of drought-resistant perennials.
From left to right, and from back to front, they are: *Stipa arundinacea, Eryngium variifolium, Knautia macedonica, Cupressus sempervirens, Sedum* 'Autumn Joy', *Eryngium agavifolium, Allium christophii, Thymus* 'Silver Posie', *Rosmarinus officinalis, Stachys* 'Big Ears'.

Trees

There are a great number of fabulous trees that are drought-resistant once established. Mulch trees regularly and liberally and make sure there is some moisture available deep down. Remember, some trees can take seven to ten years to become really well established.

Juniperus virginiana Many species and varieties are available, and are all tolerant of drought, wind and sun.

***Picea abies* 'Nidiformis'** A miniature spruce that grows no more than 1m (3ft) tall.

Cedrus atlantica This is a handsome tree, but it is not suitable for small gardens.

Acer negundo Considered a nuisance in some parts of the world, but this variegated variety makes an attractive medium sized tree.

Eucalyptus coccifera There are innumerable species of Eucalyptus, not all of which are frost-hardy. This one has dainty flowers, a beautiful multi-coloured peeling trunk and aromatic leaves. All gum trees are evergreen and some grow extremely fast.

Cercis siliquastrum This is a delightful tree for smaller gardens. It has a profusion of flowers that precede the leaves in spring. It is known as the Judas Tree because Judas was said to have hung himself on one after the betrayal. *C. canadenus* is the species known as Redbud.

Catalpa bignonioides 'Aurea' Catalpas have a very hard wood and are very resistant to pollution as well as drought.

Nyssa sinensis Both species of *Nyssa* shown here have incredible autumn foliage. They will need watering until well established.

Morus nigra A tree that bears wonderful mulberries, which birds usually find very quickly.

Nyssa sylvatica

Rhus spp Not all species are frost-hardy. Many have good autumn colours.

Parrotia persica This tree has stunning autumn colours and is a fabulous addition to a reasonably sized garden.

Pinus mugo mugo Many species of pine are very drought-resistant. This dwarf variety spreads to approximately 2–3m (6–10ft).

Robinia pseudoacacia 'Frisia' This small tree stays golden all summer. Non-golden varieties produce panicles of pea-like flowers.

Taxus baccata A wonderful example of how roots will seek out moisture. This one is so old, no one knows whether the terrain was once covered in soil, but the original seedling must have established itself on top of the rock.

Shrubs

If planted correctly and mulched well, shrubs will provide you with all-the-year-round interest and colour. Prune to shape if necessary and cut off dead or diseased shoots.

Cotoneaster There are a number of species and varieties, most of which have bright red berries appreciated by birds in winter.

Berberis koreana (top left)
Berberis 'Barbarossa' (top centre)
Berberis thunbergii (above)
Berberis come in many shapes, sizes and colours. All are prickly and all have flowers and berries. The berries are good for birds in winter.

Rosa rugosa Unfortunately, nearly all roses are great water-lovers – here is an exception. It makes a good hedge and produces enormous rose hips.

46

Buddleia davidii These shrubs come in marvellous colours and have the added attraction that insects, bees and butterflies congregate on the flowers.

Callistemon rigidus This plant has been subjected to high winds, so it should be staked. It is an unusual species, but not very frost-hardy.

Ceanothus There are many varieties, all of which have dainty blue flowers. Not all are frost-hardy and some are not drought-resistant.

Cotinus coggygria An unusual shrub that prefers full sun.

Euonymus japonicus
An evergreen, best grown in semi-shade as it dislikes getting too dry.

Euonymus alatus This has stunning autumn colours. Grow in full sun.

Genista hispanica This prickly shrub will burst into a profusion of dense flowers.

Genista aetnensis This sparsely leaved, yellow flowering tree/shrub originates from Mt. Etna, Italy.

Potentilla This small shrub is good for rockeries and comes in many colours.

Hebe Many species are available and most are frost-hardy. They come in many colours.

Cistus There are several species with attractive delicate flowers. They need protection from wind and frost.

Hypericum There are many species, some more drought-tolerant than others.

Olearia An evergreen shrub that bears an abundance of daisy-like flowers. There are several species, all of which are also very wind-resistant.

Perennials

Most perennials spread and eventually grow into large clumps, so I would not advise mulching small, young perennials with a deep layer of stones or gravel. Use something like shredded clippings (even fresh ones) with some newspaper. These will disappear in a year or two when they can be replaced with an inert mulch.

Acanthus spinosus This plant, known as Bear's breeches, has stately spires of mauve and white flowers. It can grow between 1–2 metres (3–6ft) high and has long tough roots.

Sedum spectabile This is a very drought-resistant group with many varieties, all of which are attractive to bees and insects.

Achillea millefolium This is fully hardy and there are many colours available.

Artemisia Many species are available; all have attractive silver-grey foliage, but not all are fully frost-hardy.

Eremurus elwesii 'Albus' Most species are tall with fleshy roots that retain moisture. Beware of frost.

Anthemis tinctoria Masses of daisy-like flowers are born in summer. Cut down after flowering.

Allium christophii Many interesting species of allium can be grown.

Eryngium There are many species and varieties of sea holly. Some are biennials.

Campanula latifolia This attractive spreading plant has bell-like flowers. Give it some shade.

51

Euphorbia The genus consists of many species, some of which are annuals.

Geranium You can find many species and varieties of geranium. They can form dense clumps with an array of flowers that keep out weeds. Do not confuse with the genus *Pelargonium*. These photographs show three species of geranium.

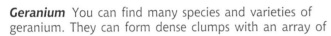

Hemerocallis Clump-forming bulbs are a feature of this perennial, some of which have spectacular flowers. Only one flower opens per day per stem – hence the common name 'Daylily'.

Iris An enormous group of perennials with fleshy rhizomes or bulbs, but not all are drought-tolerant. Consult a good book or garden centre.

Dianthus Pinks are a group consisting of many varieties and colours. Most form dense clumps and have fragrant flowers.

Kniphofia Plant properly and mulch profusely as they are not very drought-resistant.

Yucca gloriosa Many other species can be obtained; all are very drought-resistant, but not all are frost-hardy.

Rhodohypoxis 'Tetra Pink' Tuberous perennials that can form a massed carpet of flowers. Do not allow to get over-wet in winter.

53

Annuals

Annuals often only have a short time to establish themselves, so the seedlings should be watched carefully in case of an early unexpected heat wave. It is best to plant annuals as close together as possible. Also, most will not tolerate frost and many will only give their best in constant warm conditions.

Argyranthemum frutescens syn. ***Chrysanthenum frutescens*** These pretty marguerites are available in several varieties and they provide a good splash of colour.

Coreopsis Many coreopsis are perennials, but most are grown as annuals. They make a good display.

Gazania These are really perennials but they are mostly grown as annuals. They have wonderful, bright daisy-like flowers.

Papaver rhoeas
Papaver (poppies) are available in many species and varieties, both annual and perennial. This photograph shows the common wild variety which will seed itself providing the ground is 'disturbed' every year. All varieties have long tap roots and grey, hairy leaves, stems and sepals.

Eschscholzia californica These bright poppy-like flowers are loved by insects. They like poor soil.

Tagetes erecta These are not hardy but they grow quickly and make a wonderful show. Watch out for slugs.

Mesembryanthemum criniflorum These have bright colours and are suitable for very hot places.

Climbers and ground covers

Climbers are a wonderful addition to any garden; they can clothe walls and fences with a profusion of colour. Arresting effects are achieved by growing them up trees and large shrubs. Some, like the hederas, can also be grown as ground covers, as can many other perennials.

Robinia hispida This is really a large shrub, but it lends itself to being trained over trellises and arches.

Parthenocissus tricuspidata The Boston ivies acquire stunning autumn colours and like their cousins, the Virginia creepers, they prefer some shade. Both can become very rampant.

Hedera Many varieties of ivy are good for ground cover and climbing up walls and fences. Make sure they get well established.

Wisteria Although fully frost-hardy, a late frost (when flower buds have formed) can ruin all the blooms. The flowers are often spectacular.

Tropaeolum speciosum Unlike its common cousin, this variety of nasturtium has tiny leaves, flowers and multi-coloured berries. When left to its own devices, it will clamber over all kinds of shrubs and trees.

Lonicera This comes in many species and varieties. This one is a lovely fragrant climber that twines up hedges, trees and fences.

Solanum crispum An unusual climber belonging to the potato family.

Fallopia baldschaunica syn. **Polygonum baldschaunicum** This climber, known as Russian vine, is very rampant, so keep it under control!

Lamium maculatum There are several varieties. This lamium makes a good silver-green carpet with small white flowers. It prefers some shade.

Humulus Lupulus 'Aurea' This ornamental hop is a good drought-resistant climber. Hops only appear on female plants.

Grasses

Grasses and bamboos are becoming increasingly popular both for their architectural qualities in garden designs and the fact that many are drought-resistant.

Ophiopogon There are several species of this grass-like perennial which form into clumps or hummocks. They are used in Chinese medicine.

Fascicularia bicolor This is not a grass but it forms interesting grass-like hummocks with blue flowers and red bracts in the centre. It is not fully hardy.

Cortaderia selloana There are several varieties all with stately plumes. It is not fully hardy and likes full sun.

Carex secta There are several species. All are fully hardy and vigorous.

Yushania anceps There are several species all of which are evergreen and clump-forming. None are fully hardy.

Herbs

Many herbs are attractive to look at and also drought-resistant. They have the added bonus of being delicious and/or spicy and will enhance almost any salad, soup or main course.

Thymus Numerous species and varieties are available of this undemanding herb. You can make whole borders from them. Most are fully hardy and thrive in poor, dry soil.

Origanum vulgare There are many varieties of *Origanum*, including 'Compactum' and 'Aurea' (both shown here).

Artemisia dracunculus This is commonly known as French tarragon and is a must for all French cuisine.

Satureia montana This perennial is much more drought-resistant than its relative, S. hortensis, which is an annual.

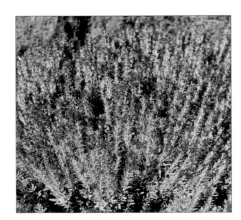

Hyssopus officinalis 'Aristatus' A culinary herb that also has many anti-viral properties.

Salvia officinalis 'Tricolor' There are many varieties, all of which are highly decorative and drought-resistant.

Capsicum frutescens A fiery variety of chilli.

Monarda didyma A native of North America, much used by the Indians as a medicine.

Vanilla planifolia If you can grow this herb, you can save yourself some money as you will not need to buy expensive vanilla pods. It is not hardy.

Foeniculum vulgare The common name for this plant is fennel. It is useful as a culinary herb, but it is also good for digestion and it is loved by insects. It likes the sun, but it is not at all fussy about the soil it grows in.

List of drought-resistant plants

Some plants are more drought-resistant than others, and the plants listed are only a fraction of the thousands that are available. Bear in mind that even very hardy plants are not always totally frost-resistant when young and should therefore be protected until well-established.

> Fully frost-hardy
> * Needs some protection
> ** Frost-tender
> *** Requires temperatures well above freezing

Trees

Abies (many species/varieties) p.20
Acacia (many species/varieties) *
Acer campestre
Acer ginnala p.37
Acer negundo p.42
Ailanthus altissima
Albizia (several species) ***
Aralia elata *
Arbutus unedo *
Bauhinia (several species) ***
Betula utilis jacquemontii
Brachychiton populneus ***
Catalpa (several species) p.43
Cedrus atlantica p.42
Cedrus deodora
Cedrus libani
Celtis australis **
Celtis occidentalis
Celtis sinensis **
Cercis (several species) * p.43
Corylus colurna *
Crataegus (many species/varieties) p.23
Cupressus (many species/varieties) p.41
Elaeagnus angustifolia *
Eucalyptus (many species/varieties, some frost-tender) p.43
Fagus sylvatica
Ginkgo biloba
Gleditsia triacanthos (several varieties)
Grevillea (several species) ***
Gymnocladus dioica
Ilex (several species/varieties) p.23
Juglans (several species)
Juniperus (many species/ varieties) p.22, p.38, p.42
Koelreuteria paniculata *
Laburnocytisus adamii
Melia azedarach **
Morus nigra p.44
Nyssa sinensis p.44
Nyssa sylvatica p.44
Olea europaea **
Parrotia persica p.44
Picea abies 'Nidiformis' p.40
Picea pungens (several varieties) p.21
Pinus (many species/ varieties) p.45
Populus tremula
Prosopis (several species) ***
Prunus padus
Pseudotsuga menziesii
Ptelea trifoliata ***
Pyrus (several species)
Quercus ilex
Quercus macrocarpa
Quercus virginiana **
Rhus (many species/varieties) p.44
Robinia (several species/varieties) p.45, p.56
Sassafras albidum
Schinus terebinthifolius ***
Sequoiadendron giganteum
Sophora japonica
Tamarix
Taxus baccata p.23, p.45
Thuja occidentalis
Ulmus pumila
Washingtonia fillifera ***
Ziziphus jujube **

Shrubs

Acacia (many species) *
Amelanchier (several species) p.36
Amorpha canescens *
Amorpha fruticosa *
Arctostaphylos uva-ursi
Atriplex californica ***
Atriplex canescens **
Aucuba japonica **
Ballota (several species)
Berberis (many species/varieties) p.26, p.46
Brachyglottis repanda **
Buddleja asiatica *
Buddleja davidii (many varieties) p.47
Buddleja officinalis **
Buddleja paniculata **
Bupleurum fructicosum
Callistemon (several species) ** p.47
Calluna (many species/varieties)
Caragana (several varieties)
Caryopteris (several species)
Cassia (several species, not all frost-hardy)
Castanea pumila
Ceanothus (several species/varieties) * p.47
Cerocarpus (several species) *
Chaenomeles
Chamaebatiaria millefolium *
Choisya ternata p.18
Cistus (many varieties) * p.49
Colutea arborescens
Cordyline australis *
Corokia cotoneaster
Coronilla emerus *
Cotinus coggygria (several varieties) p.48
Cotoneaster (many varieties) p.26, p.46
Cytisus (many species, some hardy) *
Daphne (several species)
Dodonaea viscosa *
Eleagnus (many varieties)
Ephedra (many varieties)
Euonymus (several species, some hardy) p.23, p.48
Fatsia japonica *
Feijoa sellowiana *
Forestiera neomexicana ***
Garrya elliptica
Genista (several species) p.48
Hebe (many species, mostly hardy) p.49
Helianthemum (many species/varieties)
Helichrysum italicum
Hibiscus syriacus *
Hippophae rhamnoides
Holodiscus dumosus
Hypericum (many species) p.49
Indigofera (several species)
Kerria japonica
Kolkwitzia amabilis
Lavandula (several species, some hardy)
Lavatera (several species)
Leptospermum (several species, not all hardy) *
Ligustrum japonicum *
Ligustrum vulgare p.23
Lupinus arboreus *
Mahonia (several species, some hardy)
Moltkia petraea
Moltkia suffructicosa
Myrtus (several species) *
Nerium oleander ***
Olearia (several species, some frost-hardy) p.49
Paliurus spina-christi *
Philadelphus (several species, not all frost-hardy)
Phlomis fruticosa *
Pittosporum tobira (several species) **
Potentilla fruticosa (many varieties) p.49
Prunus pumila
Rhododendron luteum
Rhus (several species, some frost-tender)
Ribes sanguineum
Rosa rugosa p.38, p.46
Rubus deliciosus
Rubus tricolor
Ruscus aculeatus
Sambucus canadensis
Sambucus racemosa

Santolina (several species) p.21
Shepherdia argentea
Skimmia japonica
Spartium junceum
Styrax officinalis **
Symphoricarpos (several species)
Ulex europaeus
Ulex parviflorus *
Viburnum (many species/varieties) p.23

Perennials

Acaena caesiiglauca
Acaena mycrophylla
Acanthus (several species) p.50
Achillea (many varieties) p.50
Aconitum (several species)
Agapanthus p.38
Agave (many species) ** p.20
Alchemilla mollis
Allium christophii p.41, p.51
Aloe (several species) ** p.40
Alstroemeria
Alyssum (several species)
Anchusa (several species)
Antennaria dioica
Anthemis tinctoria p.51
Arabis (several species)
Argyranthemum frutescens ** p.54
Armeria maritima
Artemisia (many species/varieties, some
  hardy) p.20, p.51
Asphodelus (several species) *
Aurinia saxatilis
Bergenia (several species) p.26
Brunnera macrophylla
Callihoe involucrata
Campanula garganica
Campanula latifolia p.51
Centaurea montana
Centranthus ruber
Cerastium tomentosum
Cirsium rivulare
Crambe cordifolia
Crepis aurea
Cynara cardunculus
Delosperma nubigeum ***
Dianthus (many species/varieties) p.53
Dictamus albus
Digitalis purpurea
Echinacea purpurea (several varieties)
Echinops (several species)
Epimedium (several species)
Eremurus (several species) p.51
Erigeron (several species, mostly hardy)
Eriogonum umbellatum **
Eriophyllum lanatum **
Erodium manescavii
Eryngium (several species) p.41, p.51
Erysimum linifolium
Euphorbia (several species/varieties,
  not all hardy) p.52
Fascicularia bicolor ** p.59
Ferla communis *
Gaillardia aristata
Gaillardia grandiflora
Gaura lindheimeri
Geranium (many species/varieties) p.52
Geum (several varieties)

Gypsophila (several species)
Hemerocallis (many species/varieties)
  p.52
Hypericum (many varieties)
Iberis sempervirens
Iris (many bearded varieties) p.53
Juniperus horizontalis (several varieties)
  p.38
Knautia arvensis
Knautia macedonica p.41
Kniphofia (several species) * p.53
Lamium maculatum p.59
Lantana (several species) ***
Lavatera (several species)
Leontopodium alpinum
Leontopodium stracheyi
Liatris (several species)
Limonium latifolium
Linaria purpurea
Linum narbonense
Linum perenne
Liriope muscari
Liriope spicata
Lychnis coronaria
Malva (several species)
Mirabilis jalapa **
Nepeta (several species)
Oenothera (several species, some
  biennial)
Opuntia humfusa *
Osteospermum (several species) *
Papaver (many species/varieties)
Penstemon (several species/varieties)
Perovskia atriplicifolia
Petrorhagia saxifraga
Phormium (several species, not all
  hardy) p.18
Plectranthus (several varieties) ***
Polygonum affine
Pulmonaria (several species)
Pulsatilla vulgaris
Rhodohypoxis 'Tetra Pink' * p.53
Romneya coulteri
Rudbeckia
Sedum (many species/varieties, some
  not hardy) p.20, pp.40–41, p.50
Sempervivum (several species) pp.20–
  21, p.40
Serratula seoanei
Sisyrinchium (several species, not all
  hardy)
Solidago speciosa
Stachys lanata p.41
Symphytum grandiflorum
Tanacetum (several species)
Thalictrum aquilegiifolium
Thermopsis mollis
Tradescantia spathacea ***
Verbascum (several species)
Veronica (several species/varieties)
Vinca major
Vinca minor
Yucca (several species, not all hardy)
  p.40, p.53
Zauschneria (several species)

Annuals

Arctotis stoechadifolia
Argyranthemum frutescens syn.
  Chrysanthemum frutescens p.54
Bassia scoparia
Calandrinia umbellata
Cleome hasslerana
Commelina coelestis
Coreopsis (several species) p.54
Cosmos bipinnatus
Crepis rubra
Echium plantagineum
Echium vulgare
Erysimum perofskianum
Eschscholzia californica p.55
Gaillardia pulchella
Gazania (several species) p.55
Gomphrena globosa
Helianthus annuus
Helichrysum bracteatum
Helichrysum petiolare
Helipterum manglesii syn. Rhodanthe
  manglesii
Iberis umbellata
Limmanthes douglasii
Malva moschata
Mesembryanthemum criniflorum syn.
  Dorotheanthus bellidiformis p.55
Mirabilis multiflora
Nemophila maculta
Nemophila menziesii
Nicotiana
Oenothera (several species)
Papaver rhoeas p.55
Portulaca grandiflora (several species)
Rudbeckia hirta
Salvia sclarea p.41
Senecio cineraria
Tagetes erecta
Tithonia rotundifolia
Tropaeolum majus (several species)
Zinnia elegans

Climbers

Bougainvillea (several species) ***
Campsis radicans *
Celastrus scandens
Clematis cirrhosa
Clematis ligusticifolia
Clematis montana
Fallopia baldschuanica
Hedera (many varieties) p.56
Humulus lupulus p.58
Lonicera japonica p.58
Parthenocissus (several varieties) p.56
Polygonum aubertii
Polygonum baldschuanicum syn.
  Fallopia baldschuanica p.58
Rubus tricolor
Solanum crispum p.58
Trachelospermum asiaticum *
Tropaeolum speciosum p.57
Vitis coignetiae
Vitis vinifera 'Purpurea'
Wisteria (several species) p.57

Grasses

Agropyron eristatum
Bouteloua gracilis
Briza maxima
Buchloe dactyloides
Carex seca p.59
Cortaderia selloana (several species)
 p.59
Fascicularia bicolor ** p.59
Festuca arundinacea
Festuca ovina glauca
Helictotrichon sempervirens
Lymus arenarius
Miscanthus sinensis
Ophiopogon (several species/varieties)
 * p.59
Phyllostachys flexuosa (several species)
Sasa veitchii (bamboo)
Semiarundinaria fastuosa (bamboo)
Stipa arundinacea p.41
Stipa gigantea **
Yushania anceps (bamboo) p.59

Culinary herbs and spices

Artemisia dracunculus p.60
Borago officinalis
Capsicum frutescens (chilli) ** p.61
Chamaemelum nobile
Cinnamomum verum **
Coriandrum sativum *
Cuminum cyminum ***
Curcuma longa (turmeric)***
Foeniculum vulgare (several varieties)
 p.61
Hyssopus officinalis p.61
Laurus nobilis
Lippia citriodora *
Monarda didyma
Myristica fragrans (nutmeg) ***
Origanum masjorana *
Origanum vulgare (many species/
 varieties) p.60
Pimenta dioica (allspice) ***

Pimpinella anisum **
Piper nigrum (many varieties) ***
Rosmarinus officinalis (many varieties)
 p.41
Salvia officinalis p.61
Satureia montana (many species/
 varieties) p.61
Syzygium aromaticum syn. *Eugenia
 caryophyllata* (clove) ***
Thymus p.41, p.60
Vanilla planifolia ***
Zeylanicum (cinnamon) **
Zingiber officinale (ginger) ***

Note: In the list of annuals, a number of perennials have been included as they are normally grown as annuals.

Index

annuals, planting 38

blackwater 26
butts 8–9, 15, 29, 31
 linking 12

cesspits 13
collecting water 8–15
compost 16–18, 32, 33, 37, 38
containers 8–9, 29, 31
 linking 12
 making 10

drip irrigation 30
drought-resistant plants 40–63
 annuals 54–55
 climbers 56–58
 grasses 59
 groundcovers 56–58
 herbs 60–61
 lists of 62–63
 perennials 50–53
 recognising 40
 shrubs 46–49
 trees 42–45
 watering 24–31

evaporation 9, 24, 38

filters 12, 29, 30, 31

greenwater 26
greywater 26–27
guttering 10–12

hedges 22–23
hoses 24, 26, 27, 29, 31
humus 16, 32, 33

irrigation, drip 30

judicious planting 32–39

lawns 39

meadows, planting 39
mulches 29–30, 32, 34, 37, 38, 39,
 46, 50, 53
 inert 19–21, 25
 organic 17–18, 25, 33

overflow pipes 17

perennials, planting 38
pitcher irrigation 27–28
plants, protecting 22–23
plastic, planting under 36
ponds 14–15, 30, 31
propagators 32
pumps 8, 15, 27, 29, 30, 31

rainwater pipes 10
reclaimed water 26
retaining water 16–23

seeds, sowing 32
seep or soaker hose 29–30
septic tanks 13
shrubs, planting 37
soil 16–17, 32, 41
storing water 8–15
sumps 30

taps 12, 29
timers 24, 29, 31
transpiration 24–25, 32
trees, planting 37

underground tanks 13–14, 30, 31

vegetables, planting 33–36

water diverters 11
watering cans 24, 27, 30, 32
weeds 18, 25, 34, 36, 52
wells 13, 31
wild flowers 39
windbreaks 22–23